PRESCRIBEE

PRESCRIBEE

CHIA-LUN CHANG

Nightboat Books
New York

ISBN: 978-1-64362-151-7

Cover design: Haoyan of America
Cover photography: Chia-Lun Chang
Design and typesetting by HR Hegnauer
Typeset in Bembo and Avenir

Cataloging-in-publication data is available from the Library of Congress

Nightboat Books
New York
www.nightboat.org

For my family

獻給
張明鎮
石敏束
張家雯

pre·scribe
\pri-'skrīb\

verb

to officially tell someone to use (a medicine, therapy, diet, etc.) as a remedy or treatment

pre·scribe
\pri-'skrīb\

verb

to make an authoritative ruling
be subject to legal prescription
to write before

prescribee
\pri-'skrībē\

noun

to witness unbearable negligence and make no sound
to stay sane steadily
to place music next to a pulse before a rookie serves in the military
to suppress prediction when a citizen receives the order

CONTENTS

1   Parents

3   River Mississippi

5   The Accent Floats

7   After the Prolonged Tide in the Dusk

9   Extracted Wild Cypress

11   Do Not Grow Flowers for Oxygen

12   If I Were Born in America

13   The Government Makes Me

14   Engli-shhh Isn't Yours

17   The Color of My Face

19   The Remain

20   Simpatico

21   Filariasis

22   Passive

24   Mère

25   The Scar

27   How Much Do We Trust on the Phone

28   Why Can't We Simply Love Each Other's Face

29   Upon Disrespectful Advice

31   綠繡眼 Mountain White-eye

32   The King Must Die

33   Against Nostalgia

35   My Teeth Keep Grinding at Night

36 Light on Ice

37 The Problem of Meat Eating in the States

38 The Form of Pomelo

40 My Green Card Was Denied

41 Being Poor

42 Mother Hunter

43 Winter Has Never Arrived

44 The Auctioneer Hits the Hammer

46 The Border Crosses My Beef Soup

48 The Milky Way

50 Over Lunch

53 Masculinity

54 The photographer took my photo and claimed
   I'm the immigrant dwelling

56 Naive American Boy

57 My Green Card Was Denied

59 Indifferent

60 Why I Am Not A Comedian

62 Prescribee

63 Iridescent

66 No color No book

69 Selfish

70 How to Stay Mad

71 Infusing Dry into FIDI Bay

72 Let Me Lay Down Like A Song

74 Go Back to Your Country

PARENTS

He was in love, he spent decades figuring it out, our father, who ended up spending a quarter of his monthly salary on an electronic dictionary. The sexy robot offers, pronounces, creates another man, a foreign man, a respectful man, a free tour guide.

Father said, *leave Sun-Moon Lake, come back as an outsider, witness your cousin's wedding and see the couple burn their charred love. We live next to the lake, so we are always fine.*

I buried my father too many times; each time I went deeper, his face went colder, and the signal weaker.

Father commanded, *leave before I cut the last bit of your tongue, mangle you, train you to sit and look into our eyes from the bottom of the well. When you leave, close the door without making a sound. Sounds grate my blood.*

I came to the United States for love. When men asked about my past, I replied, Father said *we must not talk about*

feelings. I practice a man coming to me by holding my breath under the water. We're repressed and they're satisfied.

She was in love, she spent decades discovering it, our mother, who ended up spending a quarter of her life performing how to dress, covering her black skull, flamed legs, and scars— milky lakes, pinky shores. She learned to be deaf when her boss came in.

I taught my mother to build her name too many times, each time she became a shalom, she demanded to know,

Have you found your love. I cut out part of my language to make love to them. I stand on the sticky floor and mop, solace their babies with homemade hugs and cuisine, endure in traffic while delivering hot soup, drive them to heaven under the rain, cook ramen through the ocean, translate bad news from the other side to comfort them to sleep, guide them on the phone and paint their nails rainbow and poison. At night, we smoke because we have endless love. We wanna be their fathers and mothers this year. To care for this land,

I dream of my babies becoming Marco Rubio and Obamacare. I slap my child's face when gene deletion affects his pronunciation.

When I smell perfume, I call home and tell them the scent tastes different from goji berries.

When I smell cologne, I call home and tell them my man is coming home next lake.

Claps. I've climbed two mountains for twenty-four seasons.
Make no decision on the dark balcony. Claps progress. Sing
a nagging song. I chose to leave after the landslide season.
When a seat picked me, it turned off the sunlight. Continue

clapping. Sarah picked five Fulbrighters up and two were
vacant. I filled in for a reason. Five of them go every month.
I go when I prey

You always receive what you pray for

not having a car. You're not mute. You're nothin' to talk
about. Not Christian. You do not slush. When's the moment
for outside groups to

clap. American roads are dark. Sarah drove us to look at
Southern culture. We picked and carved pumpkins and
repeated Thanksgiving. We pitched forts in the park. We
arrived on the top of the hill and read American Poetry.
Mosquitos chomped because we have yet to generate
antibodies. Our bodies exist for a reason. I pray for

priests to stop driving me to church's (chicken). I pray for
activities I was not allowed, flushing the toilet for free,
drowning our bodies in a fish tank (bathtub). I soak donuts,
stare at wild cats, rent in the woods, mock the continent
(land), wipe doggy hairs in a drying machine, eat roadkill, add
sugar in red tea. I chase Mr. Twain and pray that

our bodies exist for a reason. Another woman has your name.
She lives in an engraved castle. Clap her for a number. One
Korean murmured, I could have been sent to a better place.
Sarah picks you three months later.

You're recognized. You have not fought. You're (oriental)
mandarin. I'm typhoon.

THE ACCENT FLOATS

Please bear with me

I'm sorry that you're
forced to be surrounded by my voice

My lips aren't placed where they're supposed to be
The R sound eases its way out

Standing here, I annoy you,
drag you, punish you

I'm sorry

I was once your parent
who suffered escaping to the wonderland disorder

once your uncle-in-law
who died alone in an open closet

once your pet
who whined at a cryptic front door

twice your wallpaper
that peeled away through a silent,

early morning. Your mailbox has received
thousands of correctly spelled and typed news from the world

sometimes I was your blackboard
where a teeth-straightening system grew

once I was you
who sucked your mom's nipples

I'm sorry—I'm becoming a dishwasher right away

if one day you recall on a whim
please remember, we've only interacted in script

my tongue mixed too many oceans
maybe it will drown next time

my tonsil swallowed a bag of stones
on the muddy path

always flowing between terminals
my accent never takes off since

my throat has not applied for a passport
it is too thick to pass through your years

AFTER THE PROLONGED TIDE IN THE DUSK
after The Great Retreat

you come along with showers, always tramp in December.
With chilblains, you're granted giant maggots. I say, Go away,
I never belonged to you, bury my foot, and leave the cell
open

in a tiny and moist room, bed to bed on an island, the
wave flickers the sight of the dawn, cannonballs sing

after the prolonged tide in the dusk

all the places where I walk by are consumed: freckles
bridge on my back from overexposure, leeches settle on
my shoulders, my legs sweep with humidity to raise fungus,
vultures peck my forehead

under the narrow and dry farmland, seed by seed, pesticide
carries lung cancer to Mr. Veteran's mailbox, long rifles dance

I sit on the hill and have my wrists coiled with newspaper as if
I am well-known. As if my head is worth thousands of native
villages. As if my traditional movement drops the beat. Stay,

joy, as it is supposed to happen in time

You're tired, tireless, and weak. I am a medium curse. I'm
tattooed with dirt, so you escort culture. I sit on the hill and
coil newspaper into a wristband, divert my gaze to dark mode,
fold my tongue into a silk fountain, you want to drink me, say,
the cell is open. At the retreat

we are getting married.

At the wedding,   everyone dresses in telegraphs
and pain relievers. Your soldier uniform is attached with
perspiration and admonition. Documented, not a typical
penetration. Stay, joy, so I can burn you to the sun. I am all
the way naked, as a red moon

after the prolonged tide in the dusk

EXTRACTED WILD CYPRESS
after The Rootless Orchid

There were retreaters trimming their putrid roots

Root in, root out, rootless people as

Flying orchids, swarming duckweed

They lodged at the corner of the room, in the pound

Mourning, diffusing

Here are natives adopted

Trekking in the early-summer rain, for years

Discontinued their journey

To mount the base of the nation

Turning to flawless furniture

Their stems hope to be the bone of another family

Do wild Formosan cypresses remember

Their red-brown barks

The aromatic nature

How time whiffed their grains and haslets

There were retreaters trimming their putrid roots

Here are locals mystifying the roots

DO NOT GROW FLOWERS FOR OXYGEN

I spread rose myrtle and cannot understand why
the Republic of China is not located in the mainland
in order to trust a man-made system
I pass a bowl shape of the window
fulfill with eyes

listen careful, lily
people learn what it means when
loyal men sit
around the table
to discuss a slim chance

to take over
women boil streams under pajamas
at least both sides take comfort
in how the
status quo is made

to balance the system
some have split the skin
a few have hidden
most cut off tails
to survive or sign up for surveillance

watch your steps
under the clouds, dark light comes in
do not grow flowers for oxygen
they will be everywhere
seduce to be pigment

IF I WERE BORN IN AMERICA

I would be proud of who I have become
My bone would bond with the land
My nerves would begin to burn from truths

To form a nationality
I would tangle with refugees and it is not because

History makes them
History makes
A superior America
Where a killing manifesto
Had been written

To seek a phonograph to assemble
Freedom

Have I held chronology upside down
Have I traced the trail in a forgotten map
Have I enforced an agreement by diagonal law

In an inescapable
Inseparable
Inevitable saga
I stay invisible
Invisionable until

The empire murders itself
With foggy heroism
I'll volunteer to be an
American obituary writer

THE GOVERNMENT MAKES ME

lie if I want a visa. They paint me as
a bunch of aloe. Locked fluid inside
my skin. But I've become a cactus
by adjusting to dryness. Others suggest
mimicking a rose. That'd make it easier to
be picked up. No one appreciates aloe,
squeezed, swallowed, or applied
on skin in summer kitchens
only. Check the box for venus flytrap
to sign up as an immobile predator.

None of the above dare to grow roots
until the government announces
that all of the thorns build a fence
preventing connections from
another side. Thus, my answer oozing
from the polygraph is nimble.

ENGLI-SHHH ISN'T YOURS

it belongs to paradise.

Where Bruce Lee was a pan-pan girl,
sold by panglish.

Where sulfur in splashy hot springs
wasn't yellow,

it could be transparent
coming from my lips.

But bombs are owned by soldiers,
I needed to speak English

to kiss them who
bangbang without paying.

What kind of kung fu is that?

Do not purchase the company of a girl
for more than 24 hours at a time;

they seldom look as good in the morning.

English bangs the window, the coastline
flows in several transients.

This new language is a monitor's
copy and paste, in charge of

the local R & R center where the
price's kinky. When I negotiate,

pages I wrote are seared by liquid
the sound I made erupting,

as there's a bone stuck in my tongue.
Reminder: as a traitor, I need no bones.

As a server, I provide comfort: no
communication. Cold spring vaporizes.

This acquiring language has shrunk,
I wear it the way girls are waterproof.

Fact check: there are many suppliers spreading;
every second, I cover my face

beam a tale, weave a silence.

English doesn't belong to everybody and
my language is never mine.

My kung fu is learning
English to explain

the knowledge misplaced in the museum,
the acupuncture of healing,

cholera I once missed,
my fearless chieftain,

braveless mother.
English empowers me.

Wearing display devices on the conference table,
I'm trained into a voiceover.

I need to gain the most profound words
to prove to the speakers:

I'm valuable &
look good in the morning.

THE COLOR OF MY FACE

like the surging women parting and pouring onto the street, I
followed the blue dress lady, step by step

until she stopped in front of silver night and was annexed.
I am aware of myself making countless mistakes.

The lousiest voices come in with Feng Shui,
nightmares and renown.

The color of my face (in the States) isn't
just my eyes. I hope my

education is a universal disaster. The film
of my eyes is another unilateral hint.

The season of my face
is overcooked and irrelevant. Do not catch them

at your gathering table.
                    teeny, somber

pointy compass. Crashed ambiance on an unfolded
firefly. Sunburned petals, I send a box of

pastels, you summon the God of

installation. No

color represents neon. You
need to be someone else and
stay the same
ghastly
forever

THE REMAIN

The longer the building remains,
the blurrier the memory sculpts.

Only variations remain,
once in a while, rivers,
always joggers, ups and downs.

The remain of the city eats
buildings out, and converts
residents and besties to skylines.

The city is too full to preserve my body.

In order to build assets
in my womb, I hang in the
street and shadow the city.

I don't know how to deal with
uncertainty, yet my routine
sculpts a route between
new
architectures,
old
temperatures.

SIMPATICO

To advance society

display a Christmas tree after removing nests of random birds,
uprooting, cleaning the debris of leaves

wear a shirt after the young female worker sews saliva and
mucous in, folds it, and irons it with her bruised nails

chew salmon after chopping off its head, cutting off its armor
and plucking out the stomach

starve a mouse after catching it on a glue board, rolling its face
over, tearing the skin apart and putting another glue board on

dip a spoon of honey after ordering a hive online, feeding bees
in spring, anesthetizing their tongues and poisoning them to
death in the winter

drink a cup of coffee every morning after the bean picker
collects 120 pounds in the rainforest, paces on slippery bare
feet and stumbles home in the heat

swallow an egg after a hen sits without claws, breathless,
plumageless, musing about her babies

add gas to a Mazda after the pipeline transports it under the
seabed, under islands of mountains, under the highway, under
the treehouse

FILARIASIS

for Frank

Let go, you are
Fake in a green carpet
Gentle in a bombast
Stinky inside a blanket

Yesterday you went to the House of Cards with a sparrow
in your stomach. Flying above the roof, the feathers made
you cough

Let my

Honesty drive you to the purest sea
Grumpiness pilot you an unlimited outline
Hypocrisy donate your demand to a traitor

Today you arrive in the gardenia. Your vehicle, a pinwheel.
But our dreck doesn't come true. The delivery service sends
you a thorny compliment

You kidnap my insecurity in exchange for your identity
You have been to thousands of islands but have only earned
one ship

Tomorrow you will land on my chest with a slice of waterside.
You will sleep tight with my spelling of lullaby. You draw a
landscape, addressed to me, then tuck in a statue of dignity

PASSIVE

I am waiting for
The mail
Handwriting
From your left hand
Fluent and handsome

An apple appears from your teeth
 Two chairs attached to your childhood
    Three pillows steal your dreams
Four fingers as anemic as tone rings

You exist in outer space
Aimlessly walking toward another planet
The shiniest spacecraft is the chain to your glasses

I recall the moments of you
Begging for a signal

Is the shout out a howl, whistle, or mute
When you need oxygen

I ask for a cup of water
When you dance by your toenails

Soda burps
You cannot wake up on the way to a coma

A bland smile
Blare
Blasé
Blank
Beep, Beep, Beep

Crawl to you, hang onto you, step on you
Sentences are useless when I listen

Notice is a motion
Jealousy is an action

We share embarrassments
when touching on past topics

Lay on your calf
but I'm no longer contingent

Dodging my head once under your arm, avoiding those radio
stations, passing the roads alongside September, we are going
to next semester

No more melon flowers
Silent, the most dangerous arrows hide inside your hands

The way to tomorrow is to tear out one page of daylight
A dispute is not as plain as _____

Wait
Clock

MÈRE

In a conversation with someone remembering
her relatives—

To elicit a synonym, I sink in
a landscape, some strangers

have faces embedded
in the book. I echo their voice.

Their body was implanted in
air, trees, and compositions
by the farm. I sense the seed.

In the garden, we grow
arts and ants. It's a direct and
contiguous communication

to the present. We

grow up together: tangled
tainted
triggered:

We left to the city, merely
can't escape from nature.
They shower in the winds, merely
can't respond.

A quiet time to pine.

THE SCAR

He crouches to kiss my scar on my right knee softly and raises his head to sniff my moss shirt. He does not know that I look at him with an unknown sentiment. The odor of his neck, the texture of his skin and the sentences from his mouth all belong to me at this moment. He looks back at me with a pair of glistening, animal-like black pupils.

The scar is pink and dark brown. Like a little monster reborn, it roars on my body. I got it from a car accident. That year summer was hotter than any summer before. I had just come back from a southern kingdom, my body still smelling like fish sauce, sea breeze and aimless traveling. But the adults said it was the time to settle down, so my auntie found a job for me. I began a routine life like a hamster in her cage.

No one knows what happens under the sea. When the surface is calm and peaceful, something may be brewing underneath.

I started to go to sleep on time, and the food tasted like paper. I read the newspaper but pretended nothing had happened in my minuscule, narrow world. I talked politely to others and I rode my scooter faster and faster. I thought there had to be an exit to this life and I tried so hard to find it. Every morning was still a daylight maze.

I knew it was going to happen. I just couldn't expect when. I felt a part of my brain ripping to make sense, "bleeding is better than boredom." Maybe I was waiting. That morning was as hot as usual. The traffic light turned red, and I thought I had one more lucky chance. I sped up the throttle, and a row of soldiers came out suddenly. I turned the handlebar to the left aiming at the sidewalk and my scooter instantaneously slipped on the ground. Sunlight beamed into my eyes unavoidably. I lay on the ground with my wounded body when the sky was extremely beautiful in cyan. I had not seen any color for a while because I did not even think about raising my head to the sky.

After the accident, I quit my job and now I'm lying in his arms sobbing for no reason. Both of us are drunk on a bottle of red wine. He says, "It's okay, everything's going to be fine." With his deep voice, he gently calls my name. Both of us know it is a lie, but we live in this lie. And we need the lie, as when you go swimming, you need water to move through; we rely on lies, so we can keep going. It's not fine. I'm broke. I have to find a job as soon as possible or my family will be furious.

I am not in a rush. I am lying and listening for something to happen. I stare at the wall and wait for something to happen. I sit by the side of the wind and wait for something to happen. Nothing happens but the birds are singing, the kettle is emitting clouds, the bugs are walking across the wooden table, the dictionary whispers, the flowers bloom, the soap exudes a clean smell, the chairs protect me like sentries, the tap drops its tears and my scar is waiting to be kissed.

I'm tempted to hurt him badly. But I decide to stay in his arms and wait.

HOW MUCH DO WE TRUST ON THE PHONE

Knowing the poor connection distorts
The manageable truth. Not us,

The connector has no story but
Concepts, always leave a vein of

Salt inside the line. Cellphone limes &
Ashamed,

Someone must pay attention or bills. Not
Us, a mighty infinity pool between

Your voice is breaking up with—
My ex breaks away a

Landmine. Call me again
I'll be thinking about relationships &

Where can we completely trust
On lifeline?

WHY CAN'T WE SIMPLY LOVE EACH OTHER'S FACE

You really
love my face
only why
won't I be
quieter
I'm too
really
in love with
your face so
why don't you
harbor your
gross heart

Only true love cares about inside, we
are improving everyday, aren't we

UPON DISRESPECTFUL ADVICE

You can't talk to me
Like that.
You can't sit at
This table.
I was born without consent.

You're not allowed to talk to me
Like I understand.
As you can't sit next to
A mad king.
This palpable style of mine never
Wishes to hide.

I always know to
Gesture along a heavy river
Communicate while battling
Without noticing the clock
Consume lightly and behave
Vocalize the possibility of ailment

Rowdy hair
Brittle skeletons
A chameleon type of sexuality
Foreign bodies
Are dangerous.
Still, I exist without consent.

What a surprise!
Too many metaphors
You can't react
Something's wrong with
Components of my operation

I welcome all conversations
When they're flouncy
Powdery
Fair

A spark of me reflects in your
Premonition

綠繡眼 MOUNTAIN WHITE-EYE

Literal translation: Green Embroidered Eye

Nest me, please.

Fly me to your sky, I requested.
Where time stalls and
clouds are made by exquisite feathers.
They are pieces. Perching on your branch,

I heard in the den
a beak singing and a break.
I heard knocking, break fast.
I heard flipping, a breakthrough.
Here comes the peak, I heard
your brain pinkly squeaking.

In return for your magnanimity,
I invited you back to my cabin.
Revealing a need to lock the bird calls, I placed
the wing on my eyebrows.
I stitched the crown into eyelashes. The claw inside
my sunken-eye was inhibited.
I petted the tail 'til
I here what I hear.

Should not have accepted the calling,
you entered. Indoors,
docile, light-footed bone. Between you and me,
an animal is in need of a piece of
functional/fictional further/feather.

THE KING MUST DIE

I do not
trust the strength of our gods

in the most fertile land
I have seen people shredding each other apart

our body bursts out laughing by
ingesting fresh sap

celebrating spectrum in our vein
made by ephemeral subjugation

you must know I once believed in
the spirit of virility

you must know the king is my
sister and he has to die

our gods were killed by
protecting weeds and butterflies

I do not trust our gods and
all kings must die

so that
we follow democracy

underfoot
an unsuitable queen

AGAINST NOSTALGIA

Circle between somewhere of flat cypresses
when volatile sky before sum rain
dribbles before faces astray raise
your head from a dictionary
raise your hat from one and another
degree put chill consciousness down
is age a mother it's not funny yeah I
am so humid when we lie under
the sacred trees end up being a meeting
five minutes vague putrid roots there
is no construct nature she ain't
transplanted seedling

please sometimes I break you
I have been spending my entire
life preparing for leaving grey
peace off wipeout lotus unaided stages

too many tiring people one
step away from disappearing
as soon as they open windows
drip pauses typewriting
mail mechanism out melt
T-shirt I don't see
shores pepper blind do you
hear my French war is a peach
of wall war raises waves
revolution young adults hide
behind hinoki tables you don't

come to an end I am obedient
to answer I think all
I want is being flawless
teary eyes, sparkling tumors so
I go, I lie, I tree and I were

MY TEETH KEEP GRINDING AT NIGHT

The teeth keep grinding at night
my dentist suggested getting a NightGuard

or my mouth would be too flat to chew

How am I going to stop sweating
without deodorant?

Why didn't you inform me before
you stand up to leave the conversation?

Can I kick the cough away after binging a bag of lozenges?

I've been trying to find a sincere way to express
I never liked your art, but I don't

mind spending time together. Teach me:
How can my teeth stop against my will

while I'm unconscious?
I have told you my most notorious secret

LIGHT ON ICE

Listen to your body;
it has spoken. Walk one step or
several—leaps. Wait
for an intimacy. No puns
inside the flux. Do present between
both scales. This way
has the currency.

The light is closed. Guess even coral
reefs transpire now. Beneath
the light. Oceans filled with
plastic. Damage is done. Wind
in water cooling the heat. Leaning
to the slide of one eye
fish. A sad solution gains
ground. This way
out.

THE PROBLEM OF MEAT EATING IN THE STATES

is not slaughter
from where I was

I stepped on a snail still
gobbled my morning mushy mucus vermicelli

fought for the fish eyeball with other kids

the average woman kills twelve chickens in exchange for pregnancy
my cousin's chicken had eggs stolen

throat cut, thrown into boiling water alive to remove its feathers
became the nutrition of my nephew

and I love to tickle his soles like holding chicken feet
I released my artificial propagation pet into the pond

my father taught me to finish everything on my goddamn plate
shape and carry each soul of animals to hell

because he did not see a future
the only item I left was carrots

my problem of eating meat in the States is not that
the poorest family drinks Coca-Cola or

Pepsi, the meat is shiny, smooth, pinky, heavenly
beheaded and squared by a candy package

but who dares to say there's no Santa Claus

THE FORM OF POMELO

After reviewing your personal history
bilingually,
the receptionist of the clinic praised
you on your first language.
In a distant land, what you were
born with became a talent.

You often dig into spontaneous stories;
shocking surprises.
You enjoy eating the pomelo in
alien countries because it's
barely known. You're not
sure if you really like the:
Crisp
Delicate
Round shape
How it associates with the golden moon.

Or how it protrudes you from the crowd:
A rare species
An original flaw
You haven't learned to
take in the nature of love.

(Here, even tedious objects became precious simply by
disappearing)

You think about the
gentleness of your old and new
lovers. Fire pops out from their
eyes.

The sacrifice of your family. You want
Your love to come with a price and
Constraint.
You're special. You are seen.

MY GREEN CARD WAS DENIED
on October 13th, Black Friday.

I filed this application to
abandon my parent country.
Throughout nights of inspection,

a stack of paper
made by betrayal and scissors,
overgrown.

Shouting from its ice teeth
Baying to reach a bay
Pruning aged letters away

Calligraphy can no longer
recognize its own face nor
trace the night bus home

Many other stacks of paper
suppressed/shuddered by
shredders/shelters

BEING POOR

I receive hunger. I ask my family for direction:

We have to sing continually so our bodies can generate ecstasy.

So sweet it tastes like sugar and a bit like tomorrow.

We need to stay hungry for security,

speed, shed, and spotlight.

Many people are shocked by the decision I made

for saving egos, which is none and a lie.

How about we open a restaurant to keep scarcity away.

My stomach is always empty, aching for hope and risk. As

long as we still own tears, we're able to miss

the food that shows who we are. Yesterday

I told my father that I long for white rice

with vinegar. He said I'm lucky since he has never felt food

in the mouth.

MOTHER HUNTER

Even. Tricornered walls are reflected from half
of the mirror. Parents are even equally.
One and each. Some girls' long hair was hidden by
Mother. Not even. She escapes from the reflection.
Whyever she stops running. Streetlights avoid her
trembling legs. Whyever she bikes down from the
hill, I gear up to catch up. Goal: to grab that
ponytail.

I have the same name as nobody. They want to
start over. A family meets fresh means. Flesh
branches. Grandpa stole a baby from
the hospital. She stops running since. Volcano
meets plum rain. Hail meets hot spring. She builds
the streetlights so that I can replace the baby.
Pretty please pretty enough to erase. This year
I walked into grandpa's house. Mother said:
it's not here. Direction is earthquaking.

Father is a reflection of borrowing goods from
neighbors. Father is half of grandpa. Their language
is reflected by me. Not even at school. Mother
produced me then hid. Mom: you're in this house.
Come up or I'll erase/stalk/steal/delete
your child-hood-body. Now
we are even.

WINTER HAS NEVER ARRIVED

Ain't you cold. My mom never understands how I
wear only panties and a white vast while it's snowing

outside. Like every grumpy daughter, I never explain
how heaters and hurricanes sound when they crush

streets, like airplanes. Our house in Taipei never had
heaters, we slept together with heavy and puffy comforters.

Boiling water inside. As soon as I reached out my hands,
a frozen river of raindrops flowed through my back to my toes.

My cheeks confirmed, it wasn't chilly enough
we ain't dead

but my mom became the cold. She coughed at night and
sealed her passion. She has been waiting for a winter that

is cold enough to buy a new heater. Sitting under the lamp,
she asked, ain't you beautiful. 20-- is the hottest year. Her

daughter is turning American. Wearing a holiday sweater, I
tell her home is too hot to arrive in my boots.

THE AUCTIONEER HITS THE HAMMER
for John Sotheby

My ass burns northward
after sitting behind the desk for twelve hours
and hearing you shout that
free coffee is only for bidders.

John, have you heard of the floater program?
art history graduates wander to different
departments learning art things and operation,
receiving the highest minimum hourly wage,

$14 and loitering six days a week.
The job description indicates new employees
aren't supposed to maintain souls,
no eating so their bodies are yielding.

Will you apply?
Will you go to Iceland,
mother nature's so-called prettiest?
Are landscapes also fine art for sale?

John, the art handler shared that he was lonely
by eating meals at the empty round table.
I, too, love the lonesome. I cried at the
gallery because no one would visit while

floaters gossiped about the new CEO like he's
their freshly dead neighbor.
John, let me remind you of your name here
in case you try to leave the chair.

I learned to pronounce your name in ESL
classes and always mixed you up with Mary.
Nameless, none of the artists live close to 74th
street, they collect a summer in their paints

for winters passing through an undertaking.
After the 2008 financial crisis, you
focus on Asian and Middle Eastern art.
The Chinese faces twist in rage and fulfill

the lobby, not because of a bull market
nor being forced to travel nor what you
wrested from their ancestors, but because
your machine can't read CUP cards.

John, would you hire me as your assistant?
You were a book lover who stole from
libraries, I was an art appreciator and
now a stock-cannot-affordee.

John, you're dead but your spirit is up
to sell eternally, it is not fair. You're only
the nephew of the founder. Our love
won't last the length of an auction.

THE BORDER CROSSES MY BEEF SOUP
through banned drugs.

In the tradition, farmers have not eaten cattle for decades
to respect plowing, vehicles, taboos.

I've eaten steaks aka the best friend of older generations
with a silver knife set at the continental breakfast table.

To practice modernism,
my mother cannot spend time delivering the warmth
to cover my nervous system.

She folds microchips and inserts them into
belletristic hearts. Day by day,
types and sews loans on a cellphone.

To be contemporary and supportive,
the boundary assimilates,

I've taken a cage-lifter a thousand miles high
to make sure the border
is not a visible line.

The island's surrounded by the ocean,
the border still cuts across my beef soup.

They say fat local beef causes jabber & SARS mask,
I am relucent to swallow 30ppb Paylean.

Never happened in Europe,
the governments exchange a free tourist visa with ractopamine.

Finish one bowl of poison,
it won't kill me unless I'm too pushy.

THE MILKY WAY

Where are you from?

why don't you date americans. how much rent do you pay. do you live in chinatown. which one. why are you so serious. are you confused about your nationality. can you read. how long have you been learning english. how many languages do you speak. why are people so smart over there. why are you small. why don't you go back. you want to stay. don't you have a choice. don't eat intestines. why should we learn chinese if we couldn't even breathe there. do you miss your family. will they come. can you smell our freedom.

Be social. Have an English name. Talk like us. Watch the *Big Bang Theory*. Learn slang. Find a line. Wait two and a half years for a printed document.

say the word. you are one of us now. we welcome you. come back, okay. don't leave your clothes on the tree. let me be international. are you intentionally blinking. see my wounds. the lab is your home. you should be quiet. you don't fit in. is buddha the fat guy. is there more than one fat guy. who do you like more. which part. can you see without glasses. what, aren't you happy? what's wrong with us. we never expected this land to save you.

No one stares at me
but America, you are
everywhere
selling movies

train me
follow subtitles

I have removed the crumbs
in my body
in hopes of
losing and being invisible

OVER LUNCH

the managing director visits the office to eat
on a pale day from another side of the country.
He shares, "the new A.I. technology is like war.
Yet we don't know what to fight for."

I mapped my questions out
(hypothetically),
here is the war zone
I get to pick which side and
which soldiers are on my team

I must choose:
a general officer who never subverts
a spy I believe with my real heart, the organ
an army after donating their flesh, still confused
friends to sacrifice first
enemies to let go who come back at dawn
partners who can't fall asleep at the same time as me
the window gap to hide my last love letter
the toilet water tank to preserve an ID
the scientific method to die sooner
which home turns to hell, but humans stay & wear gowns
which siblings to betray
which family members not to rescue
which hand to cut off
whether to be raped or killed
whether to be raped or killed by a brother

I must buy time and ask a second question

What am I fighting for
Who started this
Who drafted the statement
What gets to stay

In war, I gamble
with numbers,
destroy the swollen dice,
repent the outcome, try again & harder still
zero people alive

In war, I pause the sunrise
intestinally

In this letter, your closest earthling
has to hold up goodbye

> The manager is not ready for the new softwar(e) while
> I have been prepared for war since I was born in
> a bombshell at the edge of the border.
> The great powers always aim for
> a small population to vanish
> in the front line.

Yet I must make a valiant effort to carry dead-hearted and order,
look at me through an x-ray, what kind of war hero will I be?
One is trapped in a low-level operator body.

> My manager wants to discuss war during
> lunch hour while contractors debate if it's
> worth fighting for a temporary chore.

Mercenaries are hired by profitable companies
to operate AI to feed their family.
Lunchtime is for sharing a can of soda or
exporting new versions of products
and realizing someone
who has refused or can't afford advanced equipment
will suffer.

Where can an SOS be sustained?
Each corner, every corner, corners, calls.
Unseen people hide in the corner, according to a random deal.

The manager becomes uncomfortable about the map;
he says, "this is too heavy for my digestion, why
don't we talk about elephants?"

MASCULINITY

The first rule of masculinity is to know men are educated,
talented and ready to kill women.
The second is to ignore the killing.

Even the nicest prince has to stay forceful to inherit the kingdom.
The second is to stay focused on his body system or weakness.

Once in a while, men visit relation-shops.
A few of them have no coins.

I, too, love to
rescue several dragons
produce organic cum
build sustainable muscle
pet armpits
iron the ambition of a fellow
navigate inspirations
glare at the mirror and reassure
not guilty for being strong

Lacking a script, my masculinity is
not your type of moon cake
not a regular potato, but a sweet potato
not a kisser, nor a guard

I don't carry shampoo around the ceiling of
the realm

I don't buzz nor hide my knees near the
graveyard

THE PHOTOGRAPHER TOOK MY PHOTO AND CLAIMED I'M THE IMMIGRANT DWELLING

inside his essential project;

I took a picture of my blood orange cocktail,
Revolución, in front of the NYC skyline and labeled
it in my album.

Never owned a cock nor overthrown any art forms,
this savory drink soured to
hen blood, truth or dare

Tweaking my cheek with the same posture as
the photographer gripped the steering wheel
securely on his imported car.

I requested of him,
Sir, I no longer want to participate since
it's dangerous to expose my condition.
The butterfly net in the same position as
the camera blocks your view. Look out!
The ladybug perched on my face is alive &
not for catching.

This male American photographer wouldn't let me withdraw
due to a previous misconception
he grasped my legs and complimented his exotic ex-wife casually

I emphasized,
I rebuff to sell my wounds or I shall be the seller who
sets a price.

He admired,
How beautiful, you're still a monster that
submits to my amusement.

Bees collect resin outdoors,
westerners preserve the time in a jar.

Cracking me to your gold fever,
insects keep shivering in the wild.
Everybody is invited to the exhibition.

NAIVE AMERICAN BOY
for 浩研

Apropos
Packing for a space tour
Frantically winking his
Glitchy goggles from an
Expensive telescope

A naive American boy has been constructing an interminable ladder

Another expat has booked his ticket to Paris

Somewhere an immigrant has swum by beating waves, invoking

An easy summer gig

Zone X blastoff

Steeping in the bathtub, I can't distinguish whether the light's
sharpened or my sunburn's
drowned

Will Amazon cede its name to the jungle?
Or it's a concession agreement for light-years away

Can NASA keep up with

Space? is for everyone
Today in America
Space is an exclusive
Crisis for landlords

MY GREEN CARD WAS DENIED

on October 13th, Black Friday.
I've been questioning

the difference between
disappearing and death.

I once wanted to die surrounded by books
in a dusty room or attic, a place

that only exists in a Western house or
children's books.

What do I know about literature, it's not a place
full of non-native speakers.

Books are innocent. They encourage me to resist, yet I find
that my application is not supposed to exist.

Why not try to dream bigger? To dream to obtain a
green card? Why not apply like the last day before disappearing?

Books are clueless. I was trained to be a tool.
Not as smart as a home device. I don't fancy dreams, in fact

I barely dream while sleeping. When another female of color said
she only has anxiety dreams, I asked around,

How does it feel to own dreams? To dream to be
a doctor? To save lives? To dream to be

a politician? To change lives? To dream to be
a writer? To impact lives? In reality,

no one lives in books or we aren't real. People live in
utensils, plates & I see containers

the only way to escape from pain is to see my body as a
vessel that fills nullity, to embrace

death, rejection, futility.
There are no people but papers.

INDIFFERENT

when people here compete, complain
& worry about their career.
Fear losing their privilege.

Because I'm the fear
the virus
the source that causes
their illness.

I can't deny that I want my host
to malfunction

while I soak their
lymph.

As I smell my tampon while
it's warm and plump because
it's my blood, egg &
it came from me.

WHY I AM NOT A COMEDIAN

We take funny as painkillers.

When we laugh together, our eyes narrow so I don't see the disappointment.

Why not also make fun of oneself when no one takes me seriously?

Being poor is contagious.

Since my rotten organs sell cheap anyway, I try numbing, I try anger, I try fidgeting.

Only laughter kindles everyone's face into a firework, blooming.

Our room becomes brighter than tomorrow.

So we take funny to survive, it's free and wholesome without side effects.

Being poor we receive fear and medical bills.

We take, "laughter is the best medicine" too seriously and can't stop laughing.

Purchasing by impulse is discouraged because mania shrivels, only jokes stay young.

But the medical report proves our jokes are made by snakes since we are ill-mannered.

I taste venom good and fast, other members have turned
purple and bone-dry faster.

To cure the disease with mean puns is temporary.

Practicing to be a primary-care humorist, I operate electric
shock to save poisoned neighbors.

Never a doctor, I'm a lab. I want to slow cook this process for
the effects to last longer than one meal.

A permanent solution is to dote, not to fool around.

But I have failed. Craving for love is dangerously addictive.
As our family has always forbidden

Addiction, we only shoot each other with additive humor to
express affection, so I have turned my mouth to a private

joke yard. In an antidote farm, I have learned to cover trauma
with lousy distraction, I jab the joke short, quick, on the house.

PRESCRIBEE

They feed us stuff.

Description: they equal traces, clomp–clomp, sizes, men &
murk, black ocean paddlers, adventurers, swallows, war losers,
curation claimers —

> *(equal has a meaning, but not within all time,*
> *feed means take, initial, seize,*
> *us is me and many preach faces, peeled skin, knives,*
> *stuff is salt, a sound, seeds, orders, THE pill.)*

This pill's small, we take them every day while running under
the rag.

We know certain orders from doctors are terribly wrong.
Because animals sense massacre coming. We have never been
to the basement or attic. We raise our heads, looking at others
who open their eyes wide. Not wide enough to be seen. Turn
off the sensuousness —

They eat people alive and replace eating with magic. Replace
magic with music without lyrics. Replace music with three TV
channels. We focus on TV and pretend not to see butchers coming.

They feed us stuff, we stay quiet, and continue the treatment.

The doctor says we ain't madwomen, we ain't crazily addicted,

Thanks to the new technology, a pill only costs eighty-seven cents.

IRIDESCENT

Staring at my face cannot make any changes

I have scowled at the mirror to see if I can be another shade

The material is more important than the final work

I hate my parents because I hate parts of myself

My personal issues come from the brightening lotion aka whitening location

Phobia when I sit in an exotic restaurant

Is a foreign menu readable or eatable

Sentences I say with my accent can always make people laugh

I am tired of those sounds

Sentences I say with my broken grammar can always make people frown

I've learned to make fun of these bugs

my lips tapered after applying teeth whitening gel

He has never heard of Tunisia

I did not know it was in Africa

It is a revolution that scientists invented airplanes

I wish I had never been to Vietnam and Cuba

It should be iridescence

How can I control my pride

Interrupting means that I need to dominate the situation

I like big countries and I cannot lie

Can I move to Paris without speaking French

Do colonial cuisines belong to the empire of recipes

At what stage does a dish complete evolution or achieve maturity

Which accent is more standard, professional and official

I want my accent to be the most sophisticated

I don't talk about diversity in a productive way

Comparison makes me feel better

It was only by sharing DNA that I decided to forgive my cousins

My appearances remain an issue in monoethnic countries

Counting where people are from in the subway, and I'm usually wrong

Bumping into a white room makes me nervous

Sitting in the middle of a brown sofa spoils my tolerance

Sipping a cup of yellow tea causes me to become blind

I check the price to see if I want to

Touch myself softly

Dye my hair sexy

Rebuild double eyelids

Get my Green Card to

border free

white flies

NO COLOR NO BOOK

-

My dad collects receipts because there are lottery numbers on the top of them. When he reads the daily newspaper, he turns on the lamp and waits to be a millionaire in the next second. My dad has only earned twenty-one dollars.

-

Idealism: Life is a box of chocolates. A person tries his best until he finds the only one that satisfies.
Realism: He doesn't like peanut butter nor strawberry truffle and milk chocolate. Nothing makes him happy.

-

golden fish swims in the sink
sunlight snatches a neighbor's wilted plant
tea resurrects in the bowl
the afternoon aligns the painting on the wall

-

Becoming French. You have to speak French with an American accent, drink French wine, eat baguettes in the morning and crepes in night, listen to Edith Piaf, walk in the rain, smoke in front of cafes, dream above the Eiffel Tower, marry a French person. It is tiring to be French so let's quit.

-

At my first group piano class, I was off-key, so I quit. I never listened in math classes. I always doodled to forget about sadness.

\-

The artists pursue beauty, chase the truth and push the possibility to the limit. The ordinaries are sluggish, flexible, smell their greasy hair and curl up in corners. The fashionistas wear flames on shirts, rivers on pants, the moon shiny inside their braids. They have conceded to suffer a bit.

\-

People who like
black are gloomy,
white are innocent,
blue are blue,
red are passionate,
yellow are sensitive,
green are dying,
grey are me,
orange are in fields.
Does color recognize itself?

\-

One time, the teacher dragged the backpack out of my shoulders and displayed to the class my doodles on the stage. I had drawn several busty girls with huge eyes, sexy gestures and mini-shirts. The kids burst out laughing.

\-

Impressionism drags me to an inner brain where it's loud, twisted, bright, humid, contrastive and layered. I am overwhelmed after I see more than ten pieces. After I sit down, it reminds me of exercise.

–

the cicada runs downstairs from a summer
the child spins the fan around
a sketchbook is full of collaged memory
flowers are dirty, they come back every year

–

Babies are adorable by their mini nails, pink lips, pliable bones, disproportionate eyes and sharp cries. They kick their feet to the sky, climb around the toy castle and hum a homemade song. We do not change much with time. We forget to learn to adore big.

–

The middle class goes to secondhand shops. Poor people go to donation centers. Free spirits wear old coats, eat in subway stations, sleep next to passengers, paint statues in the street, become friends with street animals and doodle on your wall.

SELFISH

Oh you want is attention

what a lie addressed to us

have believed both

flavorful masks and unborn religious

register for ten minutes of grass inflammation

and feel great about

when you reveal, truth contains expiration

my dentist listened to seltzer while I used to

breathe in nothing wrong with

capitulation, thirst

busy at ignorance   no time to like your curse

allow me to pretend to leave without wages

suffering comes alone, gardening mashes spring

brutal no need to be sorry

marriage without cooking a heart and caring a seed

to fathom one-way traffic signs

multiple souls flattered, slaughter habitual sorrow

HOW TO STAY MAD
Constructively.

Being angry constantly takes energy.
How do I come up with a long-term plan?

It can't occur in the living room. Too displayable, too public.
Even chairs change their practice when strangers visit.

It can't happen in the bathroom. Too much nudity, too private.
The bathtub wants a break and realization.

How about the lobby? Rage comes with embarrassment.
It can't be on the balcony. The air alienates.

Mad in my kitchen, standing.
Fostering constructive fury while

people are dying by the failure of our system,
alone.

I must stay indignant in my kitchen,
conscientiously feeding.

INFUSING DRY INTO FIDI BAY

I move into this haunted apartment too soon and the walls
slowly emanate algae. They crave salt water every night

before several wild men, standing at the corner, search for
cigarettes with smoky eyes

in the heady aroma, old ladies switch age at the sunglasses market
some fishes jump from the skyline, they grow parachutes
thousands of foreigners sell lungs and become part of the

collection in a museum of transportation
never get lost, they sleep on my shoulders and carry groceries

I inhabit this haunted apartment too quickly and the walls
slowly collect my sensation. They said don't name the spirits or

talk too much in the room. How can I prove scream, flare,
mink coat and electricity exist?
I open a pack of pink creamy cakes and it's full of ants.

have you come home lately
don't be afraid of your hands wrinkled with wet
here, have rooftops
here's gaudy jewelry piled up in the oyster bay
because you're the pearl we fish for

LET ME LAY DOWN LIKE A SONG

The anthem of this island has budded
Yet or not yet. It determines if
I can share with people:

I always enjoy handwriting in a planner,
Inserting my fingers into preparation
Inviting all possibilities from a sketch.

I often see myself thrusting into soft clouds, hallucinating.
Even relying on the solidified ground is more comfortable
Than weaponizing my sloppy vigilance.

In fact, my planner never exists:
This country has no schedule.
Clouds are intangible and hollowed.

Perhaps I'm brainwashed by my own creation.
I never told anyone that I'm a coward and can't
Count the moments when I wish to say *Oh yeah* but I'm too puny,

Count the times when I allow my anger to deluge,
Count the number of awake, asleep people,
Or compatriots in limbo. I would assassinate

For many reasons, especially for one future, but
No one should be coerced
To prove I belong.

In aerial and artificial history
I request to stand still like any Taiwanese
Mountain

Let me lay down
Like a song
That has not been hurt

GO BACK TO YOUR COUNTRY

which I would very much wish.
Not a day goes by when I don't dream of my family living
in the States & sleeping in my arms.

Yet none of them believes in white supremacy as I do

I have always believed in white people
begging for this destiny
all pale men express emotions at first sight.

Golden heroes save the universe
describe everything as war
murder with wavy hair & clean gloves.

Mental illness wears tattoos and glasses
defeats taboos as the greatest enemy.
Ahhh! Angels singing and they're all white.

My sister's chest is in pain, she can't breathe this air
she eats dishes boiled in plastic bags
we have digested too much white trash.

Her face is almost like mine

Yet I'm whiter

MOTHER! I yell dramatically
as if I were a character from Hollywood movies
staged in a little town church, I confess by a dim

spotlight on my yellow-sand-peachy face.
Someday we'll become whites
we'll drink milk instead of soybeans

mayo on chicken and beer
will burst out from our breasts.
They are creamy, rich and juicy.

We are Taiwanese

Her voice firms

My mom empties the night for me.

NOTES

Engli-shhh Isn't Yours
"Keep out of the buses or you may lose your wallet.
Do not purchase the company of a girl for more than 24
hours at a time; they seldom look as good in the morning."
—from the article "Recreation: Five-Day Bonanza" in the
December 22, 1967 issue of *Time Magazine*

The Border Crosses My Beef Soup
"The government's decision to allow imports of U.S. beef
containing a banned drug is not connected to the United
States' willingness to include Taiwan in its Visa Waiver
Program, the Ministry of Foreign Affairs said."
—from the article "Decision to import U.S. beef not linked to
visa issue: official," in the May 30, 2015 issue of *Taiwan News*

Prescribee
In 1987, Taiwan ended a 38-year-long period of martial
law, the second-longest in human history.

Let Me Lay Down Like a Song
A reference to Peter Huang shouting "Let me stand up like
a Taiwanese!" while being dragged away by security after
the attempted assassination of Chiang Ching-Kuo outside
the Plaza Hotel in New York City in 1970.

ACKNOWLEDGMENTS

I gratefully acknowledge the editors of the following platforms, where these poems have appeared, some in earlier versions and under different titles: *Neighbird* (the Poetry Project), Asiya Wadud's *Echo Exhibit*, the 92nd Street Y website, *Sink Review*, *Apogee Journal*, *Pinwheel*, *Los Angeles Review of Books*, *Vinyl*, *Hyperallergic*, PEN America, *The Tiny*, *No*, *Dear Magazine*, *6x6* (Ugly Duckling Presse), *Literary Hub*, and *The Brooklyn Rail*.

This book exists because of the Jerome Foundation, Lower Manhattan Cultural Council, Tofte Lake Center, Vermont Studio Center, Poets House, and Cave Canem Poetry Workshop. Deep gratitude for their generous support, time, and faith.

Thank you to Belladonna★ Collaborative and lawyer Z. Zac Liu for guiding my artist visa and green card application journey.

Special thanks to my dear friends, teachers, mentors, and editors for teaching me.

Many thanks to everyone at Nightboat Books for believing in me, especially my editor Gia Gonzales.

Thank you, Haoyan of America for the cover art, the author photograph, your encouragement, support, and beyond.

感激我家人一路上無條件的支持與奉獻。

Born and raised in
New Taipei City, Taiwan,
Chia-Lun Chang lives in
New York City.

NIGHTBOAT BOOKS

Nightboat Books, a nonprofit organization, seeks to develop audiences for writers whose work resists convention and transcends boundaries. We publish books rich with poignancy, intelligence, and risk. Please visit nightboat.org to learn about our titles and how you can support our future publications.

The following individuals have supported the publication of this book. We thank them for their generosity and commitment to the mission of Nightboat Books:

Kazim Ali
Anonymous (4)
Abraham Avnisan
Jean C. Ballantyne
The Robert C. Brooks Revocable Trust
Amanda Greenberger
Rachel Lithgow
Anne Marie Macari
Elizabeth Madans
Elizabeth Motika
Thomas Shardlow
Benjamin Taylor
Jerrie Whitfield & Richard Motika

This book is made possible, in part, by grants from the New York City Department of Cultural Affairs in partnership with the City Council and the New York State Council on the Arts Literature Program.